Writing Prompts and More--

WAYS TO SPARK YOUR CREATIVITY &
END WRITER'S BLOCK

Heather Wright

Saugeen Publishers

Canada

Heather Wright
wright_writer@hotmail.com

Book Layout ©2013 BookDesignTemplates.com

Ordering Information:

Quantity sales. Special discounts are available on quantity purchases by corporations, associations, and others. For details, contact the "Special Sales Department" at the address above.

Writing Prompts and More / Heather Wright. —1st ed.
ISBN-13: 978-1515031987

ISBN-10: 1515031985

Contents

Writing is the only thing that, when I do it, I don't feel I should be doing something else.

—*Gloria Steinem*

CHAPTER 1

Introduction

Writing Prompts and More is what it says it is, more than just writing prompts, though you will find 100 in its pages. Because there are lots of other routes to creativity, each chapter invites you to explore new ways to inspire your stories or break through writer's block.

Writing prompts inspire us with words and questions and, sometimes, photographs, but there are other sources that we can tap into to find our stories. I'm always looking for new writing inspirations. Every month I create new writing prompts on my blog (http://wrightingwords.com), and when I lead workshops or visit classrooms, I love helping people find new ways to discover their voice and their story.

My search for new resources is never ending, but now seemed like a good time to take stock and share what I've found and learned. I hope you enjoy your journey through these pages, and I hope that journey's end is the story you've always wanted to write.

To take a peek at my other books in this series, check your online bookseller or my website, http://wrightingwords.com.

CHAPTER 2

20 Writing Prompts to Get the Ball Rolling

Five Opening Sentences

What characters or situations do these sentences suggest?

1. The fog chilled her to the bone.
2. Why can't I come with you?
3. I could tell by the look on Bill's face that the news was going to be bad.
4. Were dragons supposed to sneeze?
5. Part of me hated him. Strangely, that part shut down while I helped him wipe the blood off his face.

Five Groups of Random Words

Choose a group of words below, and use one, some or all of them in a story or poem.

1. Peanut, wonder, branch, time, light, care
2. Bottle, label, phone, green, never, tap

3. Table, strap, gold, seat, aware, handle
4. Screen, glow, heart, switch, black, cold
5. Gem, brick, door, circle, blue, shiver

Five Titles

What stories do these titles suggest?

1. Half a Heart
2. Castle in Ruins
3. Big Brother Is Not Watching
4. Rocked
5. The Trail Leads Home

Five Dialogue Excerpts

What scene do you see when you hear these short conversations?

1. Watch out for that branch!
I saw it. Don't worry.
It's not the branch. Looks what's on it.

2. Mike's really late.
I don't know what you're worried about.
I'm not worried. I'm angry and hungry.
And worried.
Okay. I'm worried.

3. Put that back where you found it.
No.
What did you say?
I said no. I'm not putting it back. I'm not going anywhere near there again.

4. I just saw Henry.
Are you sure? He's not supposed to be here.
He was warned wasn't he?
He was.

5. I wish you would just go away.
I wish *you* would stop complaining.
And I wish we weren't stuck together on/in this (you pick a location—boat, journey, island, truck, jungle, whatever your imagination picks …).
On that, we agree.

CHAPTER 3

Sleep is a Writer's Best Friend

Sleep

In *Macbeth*, Shakespeare described sleep this way:
"Sleep that knits up the ravell'd sleeve of care,
The death of each day's life, sore labour's bath,
Balm of hurt minds, great nature's second course,
Chief nourisher in life's feast."

Burning the midnight oil only works for so long. A creative and healthy mind needs its rest. And "sleeping on it" seems to be a great way to solve problems. If your story is stuck, a good night's sleep might be just what is required to find the answer you need to move forward.

Many years ago, I worked as a branch accountant at a trust company. I had to balance the teller's sheets and the deposit to the bank every day. Sometimes, there was just no way I could get it to work. I would leave it, go home, get a good night's sleep and tackle it in the morning. It never took more than ten minutes in the morning to find the problem.

Joanne Cantor, author of *Conquer Cyber Overload: Get More Done, Boost Your Creativity, and Reduce Stress*, wrote: "For years, scientists thought that the function of sleep was merely to rest the body and mind, but recent research suggests that sleep is essential for both learning and creativity." Research has shown that "sleeping on a problem apparently allows for a restructuring of the brain connections, 'setting the stage for the emergence of insight.'" Links to the research studies and Cantor's book are in her blog, "Sleep for Success: Creativity and the Neuroscience of Slumber--Sleeping on a problem helps you find better solutions. Really."

Dreams

"To sleep perchance to dream," says Hamlet, another of Shakespeare's characters. And those dreams can lead to great stories.

The link below explains how dreams helped Mary Shelley find *Frankenstein*, Stephen King invent the plot of *Misery*, Robert Louis Stevenson imagine Dr. Jekyll and Mr. Hyde, and Richard Bach dream up Jonathan Livingston Seagull. http://listverse.com/2011/02/26/5-famous-books-inspired-by-dreams/

On Stephanie Meyers' website, she describes her "very vivid dream. In my dream, two people were having an intense conversation in a meadow in the woods. One of these people was just your average girl. The other person was fantastically beautiful, sparkly, and a vampire. They were discussing the difficulties inherent in the facts that A) they were falling in love with each other while B) the vampire was particularly attracted to the scent of her blood, and was having a difficult time restraining himself from killing her immediately. For what is essentially a transcript of my dream, please see Chapter 13 ("Confessions") of the book."

Other stories of writers inspired by dreams can be found here: http://www.pastemagazine.com/blogs/lists/2013/10/10-great-stories-inspired-by-dreams-and-visions.html

Tori DeAngelis summed up many findings relating sleep and creativity in her article, "The dream canvas: Are dreams a muse to the creative?" for the American Psychological Association. Research suggests that "dreams themselves--with their idiosyncratic imagery, colorful extrapolations on the same theme and nonjudgmental stance--model at least one aspect of the creative process, the free association that precedes actual creation."

So how can you make your dreams work for you?

One suggestion, by the team at Writer's Relief, is to write about your dreams as soon as you wake up. You don't need anything special to write your dreams in, but if you Google "dream diary template" there are lots of journal pages out there that you can download.

You also don't need to get a book that tells you how to analyze your dreams. That's for another project altogether, and might be fun, but do take the time to write down, not just the events, but the feelings you experienced during the dream. Sometimes, the feelings that are still hanging around after you wake up are more vivid than the actual events that happen. It's not often that we are really frightened in real life, but I certainly can be in my dreams. I don't have to go far to remember that fear when I put my character in danger. I've woken up dreadfully sad missing a loved one, or been very angry at someone. These are feelings that I keep pretty much to myself and in perspective during the day, but at night they get all out of proportion, and it's that intensity that I remember when I'm writing.

Do you have a recurring dream? I've visited the same city over and over again in my dreams over the years. I've never been there, but I know what the waterfront and the downtown look like and where the bus terminal is. I went from feeling very frightened to being able to say in my dream, "Here I am again" and just go with the flow. Will that city end up in a book one day? Very likely.

The drifty, not-quite-connected-to-reality phase that you're in just as you wake up in the morning is also supposed to be the best time to get out your journal and see what happens. Kevan Lee in his blog titled "The Best Time to Write and Get Ideas, According to Science" states: "A scientific study of brain circuits confirmed that this creative activity is highest during and immediately after sleep, while the analytical parts of the brain (the editing and proofreading parts) become more active as the day goes on. The study looked at morning and evening MRI scans and observed that mornings showed more connections in the brain—a key element to the creative process." Try writing as soon as you wake up and see what happens.

Renowned author, Julia Cameron, suggests, in her book *The Artist's Way* and on her website, that each morning should begin with a pen and three blank pages of paper that you fill before you do anything else. On her website, she explains, "They clear your mind. … They should be whiny, petty, grumpy …" if that's the way you wake up. She confesses that she wakes up grumpy! This is your opportunity to, as she states, "[meet] your shadow and [take] it out for a cup of coffee" leaving you much "more consciousness as you pass through your day." There are no restrictions with regard to topic and no need to be artistic. Just dump your thoughts on the page as they come to you.

Why not see what happens if you switch that first-thing-in the-morning check of your smartphone for some time with pen and paper instead. I've actually experimented with morning pages. I admit that getting the day organized (I'm a list maker) and getting rid of the previous day's frustrations has made writing later in the day easier. Some of the clutter is gone and I can get on with putting words on the page. Face it, you won't know until you try.

CHAPTER 4

Inspiration in Post Cards

Can't think of anything to write? Read someone else's mail.

No, I don't want anyone to break the law; but there is a way to find great story and poem ideas in someone else's mail. Check out your nearest flea market or antique store and see if they have any old postcards—old *used* postcards. Though ideas for stories and poems *can* be found in the pictures, inspiration awaits in the writing on the other side. These notes from real people to real people are an Aladdin's treasure cave full of humor, pathos, mystery, bravado, family life, and love.

Here are some of my finds. See what stories or poems you can conjure up from these real-life messages from the past.

One card addressed to Mrs. Arthur Ridgewell and dated 1907 reads: *I suppose you are still in Plaster Rock. Heard that Frank 1st has left you. I guess he must be a wanderer."*

Like all good story openings, this card leaves the reader with lots of questions. And when the reader is a writer, a story is bound to follow. Who is Frank 1st? (And, for that matter, who is Frank 2nd?) Why did he wander before? Why did he come back? Why is he leaving again? Where is he likely to go? The word *still* seems important to the writer. Where, other than Plaster Rock, should Mary be? What is the relationship between the sender and the writer?

A card from Vancouver dated 1911 and addressed to a Miss McLeod in P.E.I. reads: *How soon do you think you can leave College to come west? You are needed very badly as chaperone and we would be more than pleased to have you with us.*

More questions: What was Miss McLeod studying in college or was she a teacher? What kind of person would think it perfectly acceptable for a woman to leave college, head west, and become a chaperone? Why would the sender need a chaperone 'badly? Why is there no salutation to the note--no Dear...? What social milieu are we dealing with here? Is the sender wealthy and is Miss McLeod a poor relation?

The following card is posted from Winnipeg in January 1909 and addressed to Mrs. Sharpe in Listowel, Ontario. "*Just a line to thank you for the nice Xmas cards you sent. We were too poor to send anyone anything this winter as Will's work will be done this week. Things are dreadful dull and it is so dreadfully cold, about 42 below. We did not go far when it was that cold. Dick and Elsie are well. He is working steady. How is Clarence? Remember me to him. Love to all from all. Sade*"

Think of how Sade must have felt writing that her family was too poor to send Christmas cards. The postage on the postcard was one cent and though the card was dated January 1st, it wasn't mailed until the 8th. Did Sade have to wait that long to get the postage or was it just too cold to go out? Who are these people and what work might they be doing?

The card is addressed to Mrs. Fred Sharpe; then, who is Clarence and why does Sade wish to be remembered to him? What if he is a brother of Mrs. Sharpe that Sade was fond of once, or perhaps Mrs. Sharpe is Sade's sister and Clarence is Sade's nephew. Put yourself in Sade's shoes while she is writing this card or in Mrs. Sharpe's when she hears such sad news from her friend. Maybe Mrs. Sharpe is a relative of Sade's husband and Sade is hinting for her husband to be rescued from unemployment in Winnipeg and offered work in the family business in Listowel.

If you are a poet, think of the wonderful found poems that are waiting for you in these postcards. You could weave a poem like the following:

Winnipeg, 1909
Just a line to thank you
for the nice Xmas cards you sent.
We were too poor
to send anyone
anything.
Things are dreadful dull
and it is so dreadfully cold.
How is Clarence?
Remember me to him.
Sade

I paid three dollars for those postcards and have covered a couple of pages in my journal with possible ideas from each one—a small investment in inspiration. Consider what some postcards could do to fire your imagination or help you break out of one of those (thankfully rare) cement-brained-writer days?

Inspiration on a postcard? Why not? Find the wonderful stories and poems that are possible when your writer's imagination meets someone else's mail.

Try a Google search for photos of old postcards, too:
https://www.google.ca/search?q=photos+of+postcards&espv=2

&biw=1242&bih=594&tbm=isch&tbo=u&source=univ&sa=X
&ei=p1VXVc67N4XXsAWV7YGoBg&ved=0CCoQsAQ

CHAPTER 5

20 More Writing Prompts

Five Dialogue Excerpts

1. I don't believe you.
But it's true.
No surprise, but I need more than your word for it.

2. What did Peter tell you?
Not to tell *you*.
Very funny. Now what did he tell you.

3. I can hardly breathe. I want to stop.
You can do as you wish, but I prefer to keep outrunning them.

4. Have you seen Henry lately?
Yes. He seems changed—really different.
Is that a surprise?

5. Are you sure about this?
Yeah. It's not my first time, you know.

Okay.

Five Titles

1. Red Blood at Dawning
2. Brook's Challenge
3. The Tea Shop Mystery
4. Black Mountain Trail
5. Strobe

Write A Paragraph That Includes

1. A realization
2. A thunderstorm
3. A secret
4. Fear
5. Something or someone being lost

Five Opening Sentences

1. Happiness for my dog is a long walk. For me, at night, in February, in the snow—not so much.
2. Yesterday was completely forgettable. I mean that. I don't remember a thing.
3. It's about time!

4. The next time I get asked to volunteer for something, I'm saying "no."
5. The coyotes were restless tonight.

CHAPTER 6

A Little Self-Reflection

What are you already interested in?

Aside from your writing, what are your other hobbies and interests? If you take a look at the current publications in mystery and romance fiction, you'll see authors who write about everything from quilting, to crossword puzzles, to bookstores, yarn stores and bakeries. They provide insights into their passions along with recipes and knitting patterns and their characters still solve a mystery or fall in love—or both.

Can you think of a way to incorporate what you love into your stories? If you do reenactments, or know someone who does, you have access to a wonderful source of historical detail that could be the basis for an historical novel, a sci-fi time travel story or a mystery or romance or even spy thriller using the historical setting as a backdrop to the story.

What have you already done?

You already have a warehouse full of experiences that you can tap into for your stories. What did you do as a child in the summer? Did you go to camp? Hold bike races? Tell ghost stories? Invent your own games or kingdoms? Did you play baseball or Robin Hood or pretend you were a certain group of Ninja turtles? Use your memories to fuel a story.

What smells do you remember? Did you go to the street fair or state fair and smell candy floss and popcorn? Did you go to church or the library? What were those places like? Did they have a special smell or texture in the book covers, hard chairs, pews, kneeling pads, candles? What noises did you hear at night through your bedroom window? Traffic or people talking on the street? Cicadas in summer? You can use all of these sensory details to bring your stories to life.

Where have you been?

Think about the jobs you have had. Have you had the job from hell or worked for the craziest person in the world? Do you have any stories about weird customers you served or the time the fire alarm went off or the basement flooded? Why not use some of those people or situations to spice up a story?

Or play *what if* and see what happens. What if you found a time travel portal in the basement of your building? Or a secret laboratory where there should have been an employment agency? Or one of your clients at the bank passed you a note with her deposit that says she's been kidnapped and asks for help?

Where have you traveled? Your destinations don't have to be exotic. Anywhere where you experienced something new or different from your normal day-to-day routine will do. Have you visited a family farm or your brother's dorm room? What interesting life forms and smells did you encounter in these locations? Have you traveled to other cities or historical sites on school trips or with family? Apply some what-ifs to these locations or to the trip to these locations.

What if your car broke down on the way to the Grand Canyon? What interesting characters might stop to help? What if it were near closing time in one of those historical villages, where the characters dress up and live there as if it were a particular time in history. Suddenly, a violent storm sweeps through and floods the parking lot so that the few remaining visitors have to live like pioneers for a couple of days until they can leave. What if you dislodged a rock or knocked over something and discovered a rare artifact? What if you found or heard a message from the past while you were alone in one of these locations?

What can you do?

Can you drive a car, ride a bike or a horse, sing, dance, pitch a tent, fish, run, build a car, dismantle a computer, bake amazing cookies or prepare gourmet meals, throw a football or hit a baseball, survive grad studies, return to school for upgrades, have a profession that requires special skills and knowledge, raise your children--which requires a skill set and range of knowledge like no other profession? You get the idea. You might not think that these skills are very interesting, but they can still open doors to a story or provide a setting, skills, or knowledge that your antagonist might need to solve a problem.

You can play *what if* with these ideas, too. Perhaps taking French cuisine cooking lessons is where two people meet and fall in love. While camping, people get separated while paddling on a lake during bad weather and seek shelter on different islands. A student uncovers a cheating ring, but is afraid to say anything because she needs the course to get a new job, your hero coaches little league and great hand/eye coordination is needed for a suspenseful rescue. Because you're a mom or a grandmother, you keep strange things in your purse that others don't have, but that can help in a crisis on a broken down bus.

What Don't You Know?

--or, rather, what do you wish you knew? Have you always wished you could live in France or in a different time period or meet Marco Polo or a famous spy or the chairman of a bank? Research and imagination are the keys to making those wishes come true.

There is so much information available today on the Internet, and in good old-fashioned books in the library, that there's no reason why you can't explore what you are interested in to your heart's content. Believe me, your local librarian will be more than happy to help you find exactly what you are looking for.

I'm a big fan of things medieval and have set two historical romances and a set of middle reader mysteries in that time period. (Nope they're not finished yet—but in the next year, I'm hoping ….) I love the challenge of having my characters solve their problems without benefit of smartphones or automobiles.

I'm thinking of another series set in my hometown about forty years ago. Even though I was around then, I still have to do research. Memories can be tricky.

Explore what you don't know, and see what stories might turn up. Sometimes looking at facts is a great way to stir your imagination.

CHAPTER 7

The News

Make sure you go beyond the Yahoo celebrity headlines and check out your local newspaper or one from another part of the country or the world and see what you can find. There are lots of stories waiting to be turned into something special and unique by you. A friend of mine wrote a book called *Wild Dog Summer* based on two small news story clippings that she kept in a file along with many others. One was about the death of a small town teen in a drunk driving accident, and the other story was about the increasing number of wild dogs roaming rural Ontario.

Here are two samples of news stories I found today and how the stories might be linked:

1. A story about a company in Pakistan that sells fake degrees and diplomas from web-based high schools, colleges and universities around the world: "Fake Diplomas, Real Cash: Pakistani Company Axact Reaps Millions" by Declan Williams http://www.nytimes.com/2015/05/18/world/asia/fake-diplomas-real-cash-pakistani-company-axact-reaps-millions-columbiana-barkley.html?ref=todayspaper&_r=0

A story focusing on recent government trade initiatives and taking a close look at Galesburg, Illinois, a formerly thriving manufacturing centre. "Perils in Trade Deals When Factories Close and Towns Struggle" by Benjamin Applebaum

Story 1: What would happen if several people from a recently closed manufacturing company used part of their severance to purchase degrees in various areas of expertise so they could apply for a bank loan in another state to create a new successful company? What if the company is a huge success, and then the owners are blackmailed by someone who knows their secret. What if they decide to murder the blackmailer to keep their past a secret?

Story 2: What if the expert brought in to help a family business adapt to the changing economy. The expert has fake credentials, some financial problems, and doesn't want his or her secret to come out. The expert is bribed/blackmailed to give the company bad advice so that it will fail instead of thrive. Its closing will benefit someone who wants the company's land or assets and doesn't want to pay a lot for them. In spite of the fake credentials, he or she has given good advice to companies in the past. The problem is complicated by the fact that he or she has fallen in love with one of the business's owners.

The following stories are from my local paper.

A former city landmark hotel and its neighboring building are about to be demolished. "Mayfair Demolition to Begin Wednesday"

A throw-back-Thursday article about the King Street celebrations to celebrate VE Day. These celebrations would have taken place right outside of the hotel and other building that is going to be demolished. #TBT May 7, 1945: "Noisy, Flag-Waving King St. Crowds Celebrate Victory"

This is my *what if*: What if someone hid something in the
hotel during the noisy 1945 celebrations, and it's found when
the building comes down? What could be hidden? A diary, a
body, a coded message, a gun... up to you! What other *what ifs*
can you come up with?

You get the idea now, so think about creating a file of your
own with news stories that capture your interest. Look through
your collection when you need some inspiration and see where
your imagination takes you.

CHAPTER 9

20 More Writing Prompts

Five Opening Sentences

1. I know what yellow police tape means, but I still have to get into that building.
2. Put that down. It's mine.
3. Grey barn. Red roof. Not everyone's idea of a nightmare, but it was mine.
4. A row of tall, dark pines cut through the field.
5. The car swerved but not soon enough.

Five Groups of Random Words

Choose a group of words below, and use one, some or all of them in a story or poem.

1. Tree, follow, bar, light , path, door, hollow
2. Line, sign, solitary, blue, glimmer, track
3. Call, strange, grey, hold, box, monument
4. Centre, shudder, willow, clouds, vast, no

5.   Tower, west, ditch, pain, billow, water

Five Questions For You and Your Characters

1. Describe the one place you never want to see again. Describe the one place that your character never wants to see again.
2. Where's your ideal spot to relax—on your favorite chair, in front of a fireplace, on a beach, by a river with a fishing rod in your hand? Where would your character choose? Why?
3. Unless it was on the advice of a doctor, what dietary choice would you never make? (Give up chocolate, go vegan, eat meat, no alcohol, no carbs?) What would your character decide?
4. Is there someone in your life with whom you feel you have unfinished business? If you could meet that person again, what would you say? What is your character's unfinished business? What would he or she say?
5. What's your favorite TV show on now. What was your favorite show when you were a kid? Why do/did you like these programs? What TV shows would your character choose and why?

Write a Paragraph That Includes

1. A buzz and a hum
2. Listening

3. Someone yelling
4. A fall
5. Something small

CHAPTER 8

Get out the Pencils, Crayons and Markers

Drawing and Coloring Pictures

Before they became popular, I was already coloring pictures in books as a way to clear my mind before getting creative. It happened by accident. I used to love to draw when I was a kid. I thought it might be fun to try again, so I bought *The Complete Idiot's Guide to Drawing*, which should give you a clear idea of my talent level. The book is full of drawing exercises for freeing your creativity and silencing the 'critical voice' that lurks inside your head, waiting to talk you out of even trying.

Coincidentally, I was playing with one of these exercises before some precious writing time and, when I began to write, my fingers flew across the keyboard. I've tried this again and again with the same result. I realized that I had found a way to create the inner quiet that I needed to write. When I draw, I'm incapable of thinking about anything except where my pencil is going next. Everything else disappears and the critic is silent.

If you're worried that your attempts to draw a picture would make your critical voices unite in a volume rivaling a room full of pre-schoolers with free ice-cream, grab a coloring book and color a picture. Just choosing colors and concentrating on staying in the lines can be a very quieting experience. As in drawing, the world slips away for enough time to quiet the voices and let your creativity emerge.

Dover publications (http://store.doverpublications.com/by-subject-coloring-books.html) has a great collection of coloring books that I've enjoyed using over the years, and now they offer a range of Creative Haven® coloring books marketed to adults. Google "free coloring pages for adults" and you'll find lots of printable choices and some that you can color using your computer. Adult coloring books are hugely popular now, so you'll find them in most bookstores and online.

If you have Adobe Photoshop Elements or another similar program, you can make coloring pages from your own photographs. Open the photo you want and apply the photocopy effect to get an outlined drawing that you can colour. Here's a sample.

So, when you need to silence those critical voices inside that keep telling you that you can't write, or that that sentence stinks, or that are asking why you aren't smart enough to come up with a better idea than that one, get out the crayons, markers, gel pens, whatever, and draw.

Maps

In *How to Write Science Fiction and Fantasy*, Orson Scott Card describes an evening when he sat down to watch TV and doodle a map on some special paper that he'd found. When he finished a few days later, it wasn't a map of a country with mountains and cities, it was a walled city with several gates in its walls. Only one wall didn't have a gate. It had two towers but "no gap between the two towers that guarded it." The mystery of missing gate and possible solutions stayed in his imagination and much later and after many other influences (news stories about conjoined twins, the novels of Mary Renault, a student workshop on the limits of magic, and more) he was finally able to begin writing *Hart's Hope*.

Consider doodling a map, too. I've used this exercise with writing students, having them draw a map and then think of a story they can set there afterwards. It doesn't have to be the map of a country or continent. It can be a city or a neighborhood, or a spaceship, or the interior of a haunted house or a castle. Don't worry about your drawing skills, just have fun and see where pen and paper take you.

Change Your Writing Tools

You are hot-wired to create with pencil and paper. That's how you started drawing your first pictures and writing your first stories. Sometimes just changing your writing tools can open doors to stories.

I invent new writing prompts every month for my website. I don't think I've ever written them on my laptop first. My ritual for brainstorming these prompts is to get out the journal, a nice pen, and make a cup of tea or coffee. I leave the desk and find a comfy chair by my fireplace in the winter and outside in the summer. In a different setting and with different writing tools, the words flow.

When I'm stuck, the best thing I can do is walk away from the keyboard and get out the pen or pencil and paper. A trip to a coffee shop doesn't hurt either. If your writing is stuck, try the same thing. I encourage you to buy a journal or a notebook for these times. You're a writer. A journal is part of the equipment. Get one that inspires you to have fun, be messy, and take risks. If it's too fancy, you might not want to "spoil" it by sloppy handwriting or crossing things out or drawing arrows everywhere. My journals are messy. I also don't write on the first two pages, so that the pressure is off to make the first page count. I check dollar stores for packages of 3 or 4 small journals that I can split among my various handbags, knitting bags, computer case and briefcase. They're a small investment, but they give me another option than only being able to check Facebook and my email on my smartphone when I'm waiting at the dentist's office.

CHAPTER 10

Get Moving

Walking and Mundane Activities

Researchers have confirmed it—walking boosts creativity.

And for those of you in climates like mine, where for several months a year walking outdoors is at the least uncomfortable and at the worst treacherous, a treadmill will do just fine. A 2014 research report, "Give Your Ideas Some Legs: The Positive Effect of Walking on Creative Thinking" by Marily Oppezzo and Daniel L. Schwartz of Stanford University produced some interesting results as explained by May Wong in her article for the Stanford Report. " 'I thought walking outside would blow everything out of the water, but walking on a treadmill in a small, boring room still had strong results, which surprised me,' Oppezzo said."

Oppezzo and Schwartz wrote, "People have noted that walking seems to have a special relation to creativity. The philosopher Friedrich Nietzsche (1889) wrote, 'All truly great thoughts are conceived by walking' (Aphorism 34). The current research puts such observations on solid footing."

The report also shows that the creative effects last even after you sit down afterwards. If this isn't a good reason to get moving when you need to break through a plot problem or find an idea for a story, I don't know what is. Since the writer's job usually means spending a lot of time sitting, it's good to know that creativity can be affected positively by movement. I, for one, will be moving a lot more. And since exercise also helps me sleep better, this is definitely a win/win. To read about other creators and writers (Dickens, Darwin, Beethoven) who did a lot of walking, check Craig Dowden's article for the *Financial Post*: <u>Steve Jobs was right about Walking</u>.

Agatha Christie wrote, "The best time for planning a book is while you're doing the dishes." Consider using that boring time when you're unloading/loading the dishwasher, or mowing the lawn or cleaning bathrooms as creative time. I have a friend who actually likes cleaning her house. (I avoid reading her Facebook posts on Fridays.) My attitude is a lot closer to Erma Bombeck's, "My idea of housework is to sweep the room with a glance."

Go to the Library

Wander the shelves in your library or local bookstore. If you haven't looked in the non-fiction shelves lately, explore a section and see what's there. It's fun to find out what topics other people are interested in or are experts in.

I once found a book on the origins of nursery rhymes. Some rhymes, like "Ring Around the Rosie", turned out to be based on pretty gruesome events. Maybe I could write a mystery series with each murder connected to the original origins of the nursery rhymes. (Hmmmm. That's not such a bad idea.) Maybe you'll find a book about Tibet. Look at the photos of the people, and the animals, and the landscape. What if one of your characters came from there? How would he or she cope with living in your town? Or what if your character had to live in Tibet after having only lived in a big city?

If you visit the library or a bookstore with a friend, make sure that each of you takes several small pieces of paper and writes down a book title on each. Put them in a paper bag or an envelope. Then each of you draws out one of the small pieces of paper and the title written on it is the writing prompt for the day.

While you're at the library, check the most current releases. I will never suggest that you write only to follow a trend, but have you looked to see what's being published now? Maybe there are genres of stories out there that you haven't even considered before. Maybe your mystery novel could use a little romance. Maybe your epic fantasy could use a little mystery. Maybe your techno thriller could use an alien from outer space.

While you're at the library, do one last thing. Read. Read to be inspired by great writing. (Or, read to assure yourself that you can do better!) Reading will accomplish one important purpose; it will make you escape to a place outside of your own worries and concerns, giving your brain a break from wondering where your next words are going to come from. Sometimes that's just the breather you need to get back to writing your own stories.

CHAPTER 11

Final 40 Prompts

Nine Opening Lines

1. Parker Westmore was a pig.
2. We thought we were alone until the glass shattered.
3. Mackenzie hated knives.
4. Do you think I'm guilty?
5. The walls of the cave glistened in the torchlight.
6. What do you mean Henry is missing?
7. I wasn't mad, really.
8. A book fell from the shelf.
9. Claire snuffed out the candle.

Six Questions for You and Your Character

1. What music do you like to listen to while you're driving? Writing? Working? Relaxing? Does your character listen to music? What would he or she listen to in the above circumstances? If your character is from a time period where the above doesn't apply, does music play a part in his or her life? Is it played at parties, street fairs, in the

home? Does your character play an instrument or sing? How does music make him or her feel?

2. What TV character is most like one of the characters in your book? How are they the same? How are they different?
3. What fact about your character's life would your character not want anyone to know?
4. What kind of party to you prefer? Casual, quiet and formal with cocktails, noisy with lots of music, barbeque, formal dinner? Why is this type of party your favourite way to hang out with friends? Answer the same question for your character.
5. Are you a good liar or is it impossible for you not to tell the truth? Do you have a character that has lied—or not? How has your character justified lying or deciding to always tell the truth? How does your character feel about lying whether he or she is doing it or someone else is?
6. What country or city have you always wanted to visit? Why is this place so appealing to you? What would you do there that you can't do at home? Answer these questions for your character, too.

Five Titles

See if you can think of a story to go with one of these titles?

1. The Message is Clear
2. Storm
3. Red Season
4. Through the Window

5. The Third Shadow

Write a Paragraph that Includes

1. Something being broken
2. A funeral
3. A flat tire
4. A mysterious text message
5. A campfire
6. An airplane

Five Groups of Random Words

Choose a group of words below, and use one, some or all of them in a story or poem.

1. Goblet, box, wing, blue, open, see
2. Yell, jump, wall, crown, sky, street,
3. Sunday, table, one, flame, letter, steal
4. Mud, ladder, stop, crack, help, high
5. Music, bridge, phone, eyes, wave, pierce

Dialogue Excerpts

1. I love your photographs.
Thanks.
I recognize everyone except her. Who is she?

2. You got a letter? A real letter?
Yes.
Who from?
Aunt Helen.
But I thought she was dead.
Apparently not.

3. You look frozen. Come and sit by the fire.
Thanks.
Now. Tell me what happened.

4. You went out with who?
Arthur.
But why?
He likes me.
So does your cat!

5. Do you recognize that voice?
Sadly, I do.
Do we have time to get away?
No.

6. You're late.
I told you not to expect me until nine.
It's eleven. And it's Tuesday.

7. You're going too fast.
We need to get away.
I know. But I'd like to make it in one piece.

CHAPTER 12

Last Words

Any Time of the Year Resolutions

With every new how-to-write book and journal that I buy, I make a bunch of promises: *This time I will do more writing. I will get the book finished. I will write every day.* You get the idea.

I'm not going to discourage you from setting goals, but I am going to suggest a couple of strategies for meeting them.

1. Small bites

I'm sure many of you have read Anne Lamott's book, *Bird by Bird*. It's an inspiring book and it does remind you that the way to get a project done is to work on one small piece at a time.

Writing time doesn't have to come in large chunks either. You really can write something worthwhile, even if you tackle it in 10-minute increments. Though the advice in Gregory Semenza's blog post "The Value of 10 Minutes: Writing Advice for the Time-Less Academic" is addressed to grad students, it applies to me and to every other writer I know. He clearly explains the benefits of using 10-15 minute periods of time to make progress on current writing projects. Like everyone else, when presented with a free 10 to 15 minutes, Semenza states, "My first inclination at such moments is to watch YouTube or check Twitter. That's because these activities are less intellectually demanding than the ones, which, I've, been led to believe, require considerably larger chunks of time and more sustained focus. Procrastination thrives on such assumptions."

Well, I'm an expert at procrastinating and thinking that there's no point in bothering to write for ten minutes when I'm sure that I have a clear three hours tomorrow. Well, guess what doesn't happen "tomorrow." Exactly! Those three hours simply disappear. If you're looking for places to find those extra 10 minute writing times, Jennifer Blanchard's blog has lots of suggestions: "17 Ways to Find 10 Minutes to Write."

2. Mini Habits and Writing Every Day

The daily writing habit is a tough one to maintain. Kristi Holl's blog, "No Motivation or Willpower? A Simple Solution", opened my eyes to an option that I never would have considered-- mini habits. Inspired by Stephen Guise's book, Mini Habits: Smaller Habits, Bigger Results, Kristi experimented with setting a mini-writing goal for herself: "write 50 words a day." That means that on an absolutely terrible day, when she's on a deadline for another project, or it's flu season, or she has to take care of a grandchild, the daily writing goal can be accomplished. A couple of sentences and she's done.

The benefit of mini habits is that once you've accomplished your goal, you often keep going, writing more than you planned. Setting a goal for 1000 words a day leaves me checking the word count and playing solitaire and dragging the writing of those 1000 words out for so long that, when I'm finished, I feel exhausted, and resentful of the time I've lost. I'm also dreading repeating the same thing tomorrow. However, I *can* write 50 words and the daily writing habit is being built one small step at a time. **And a daily writing habit will get a book written**

---

3. Be Kind to Yourself

Stuff happens. Forgive yourself when you don't make your goal or you miss a day of writing. Writing is a lonely job. Your only partner in this enterprise is you. When you're busy criticizing yourself stop and see if the words you are using remotely resemble what you would say to a friend who had slipped off her diet for a day, or wrote a weak ending to her story, or skipped his usual exercise drills. Remember to be as kind to yourself as you would be to your best friend. You deserve nothing less!

===

I wish you every success with your writing and hope that you found some inspiration for new stories and characters in these pages.

Thank you for taking the time to explore *Writing Prompts and More: The Journal*. If you enjoyed it, please consider telling your friends or posting a short review. Word of mouth is an author's best friend.

Thank you,

Heather

http://wrightingwords.com

ABOUT THE AUTHOR

Heather Wright is a busy freelancer, children's writer and part-time professor. As a freelancer, Heather has worked for educational publishers, non-profits and agencies. Her feature articles, profiles and promotional copy have appeared in local and national publications.

She loves research and has enjoyed writing many stories with historical settings for *Kayak: Canada's History Magazine for Kids*. Her books for middle readers and teens include *Sherlock Holmes and the Orphanage Mystery, Writing Fiction: A Hands-On Guide for Teens, Writing Fiction: A Guide for Pre-Teens, The Dragon's Pearl,* and *The Dragon's Revenge.* All are available at online bookstores.

She is currently finishing a series of short how-to books for business communication, soon available on Amazon and other online booksellers. Titles include *A Quick Guide to Writing Better Emails, A Quick Guide to Better Presentations,* and *A Quick Guide to Better Telephone Skills.*

Heather enjoys working with writers of all ages and loves to visit classrooms to teach writing skills and to talk about various aspects of the writer's life. She runs teen writing workshops at her local library and at art camps, and has also created presentations and workshops for conferences and the public.

Her website, **http://wrightingwords.com,** hosts her blog and lots of resources for teen and pre-teen writers and their teachers.